BEYOND PLEASED

WORKBOOK

Customer Service Strategy

For Entrepreneurs

By Theresa Casey Hayes, MHRM

Beyond Pleased Workbook: Customer Service Strategy for Entrepreneurs

Copyright © 2019 by Theresa C. Hayes

E-mail: Theresa.Hayes@yahoo.com

Website: www.theresacaseyhayes.com

Printed in the United States of America.

Get It Done Publishing, LLC., Stone Mountain, GA 30088

www.getitdonepublishing.com

ISBN: 9781712533703

All rights reserved. No part of this book may be used or reproduced, stored in a retrieval system, or transmitted in any form or in any manner whatsoever without written permission except in the case of brief quotations embodied in critical articles or reviews.

This book is designed to provide accurate and authoritative information about the subject matter covered. It is sold with the understanding that there is not a professional consulting engagement. If legal or other expert advice or assistance is required, please seek a licensed professional in your area.

This workbook is a complement to the book entitled "Beyond Pleased" Customer Service Strategy for Entrepreneurs. Please purchase the book to gain a better understanding of the workbook.

This workbook is designed for you to think about your own business venture and what systems you can put in place to help gain and retain your customers.

TABLE OF CONTENTS

DEFINING YOUR CUSTOMERS 1

WHAT ARE YOUR SERVICES AND PRICES? 5

BASIC SERVICE KNOWLEDGE 8

LOYALTY TO THE OLD: REGARD FOR THE NEW ... 12

CUSTOMER SERVICE ETIQUETTE 17

PRATICE PROFESSIONALISM 20

GOING THE EXTRA MILE 23

SYSTEMS TO RETAIN CUSTOMERS 27

CONTINUED EDUCATION 31

ANSWER KEY 34

CHAPTER 1

DEFINING YOUR CUSTOMERS

1. What do you aim to learn from this book?

   _____

   _____

   _____

   _____

2. Defining your customer is very _____ to the success of your business.

   a. bad

   b. crucial

   c. detrimental

   d. annoying

DEFINING YOUR CUSTOMERS

3. Why is making a painstaking decision in your business important for your customers?

   _____

   _____

   _____

   _____

4. Who are the potential customers for your business?

   _____

   _____

   _____

   _____

5. In every business, the aim is to make _____.

   a. customers

   b. friends

   c. profits

   d. interest

6. How do you prioritize satisfying your customers in your business?

   _____

   _____

   _____

   _____

7. How do you sustain the goodwill of your customers?

   _____

   _____

   _____

   _____

8. Your target market in your business are:

   _____

   _____

   _____

   _____

DEFINING YOUR CUSTOMERS

9. What drives your line of business?

   _____

   _____

   _____

   _____

10. With your kind of business, how do you think you can get referrals?

    _____

    _____

    _____

    _____

11. What sphere of influence does your business currently have?

    _____

    _____

    _____

    _____

Chapter 2

WHAT ARE YOUR SERVICES AND PRICES?

1. Your profitability is _____ on defining your success.

    a. great

    b. dependent

    c. good

    d. poor

2. What are your specializations?

    _____

    _____

    _____

    _____

3. The reason for offering specific services is for _____ And _____.

WHAT ARE YOUR SERVICES AND PRICES?

4. What is the outline for your services?

   _____

   _____

   _____

   _____

5. What are the specific services you render?

   _____

   _____

   _____

   _____

6. What are the factors you consider before establishing a price for your services?

   _____

   _____

   _____

   _____

7. How do you offer excellent customer delivery in your business?

   _____

   _____

   _____

   _____

8. What incentives do you give your customers to keep their business?

   _____

   _____

   _____

   _____

Chapter 3

BASIC SERVICE KNOWLEDGE

1. What should be your values as an entrepreneur?

   _____

   _____

   _____

   _____

2. In building your brand, you need _____ and _____.

3. As an entrepreneur, one of the values you need to uphold is _____.

   a. training

   b. action

   c. intelligence

   d. commitment

4. Describe how you express dedication to your business:

   _____

   _____

   _____

   _____

5. If you want to serve customers well, you have to uphold the value of _____.

6. What are the proactive measures you should take for your business?

   _____

   _____

   _____

   _____

7. Being proactive requires _____.

   a. knowledge

   b. critical thinking

   c. personnel

d. money

8. What are you doing differently in your business to stand out against the norm?

_____

_____

_____

_____

9. How are you preparing for the future of your business as an entrepreneur?

_____

_____

_____

_____

10. In what way, do you accommodate the views of your customers?

_____

_____

_____

_____

11. Your staff ought to be aware of your _____ and _____ of your business.

Chapter 4

LOYALTY TO THE OLD: REGARD FOR THE NEW

1. _____ makes a business thrive.

    a. Advertising

    b. Money

    c. Loyalty

    d. Intelligence

2. How do you sustain your existing customers as an entrepreneur?

    _____

    _____

    _____

    _____

3. Business service should be a personal interaction between _____ and _____.

4. How do you make customers relish the business experience?

   _____
   _____
   _____
   _____

5. How do you make your business attractive and appealing to customers?

   _____
   _____
   _____
   _____

6. In sustaining a business relationship, learn to ask_____.

   a. details

   b. interests

   c. questions

   d. hobbies

7. The way to get better in sustaining business relationship is by _____ and _____.

8. How do you get feedback from your customers?

   _____
   _____
   _____
   _____

9. How do you attract new customers?

   _____
   _____
   _____
   _____

10. How do you follow-up with customers?

    _____
    _____
    _____
    _____

11. How good your service would be is dependent on two factors: _____ and _____.

12. What is the best way to handle complaints as an entrepreneur?

   _____
   _____
   _____
   _____

13. What is the right attitude towards following up on existing clients?

   _____
   _____
   _____
   _____

14. How do you retain customers in your business?

   _____
   _____
   _____
   _____

15. How do you handle issues that pertain to your customers and staff?

_____

_____

_____

_____

Chapter 5

CUSTOMER SERVICE ETIQUETTE

1. How do you listen to your customers?

   _____

   _____

   _____

   _____

2. Why do you have to sample the opinion of your customers?

   a. To know if the service would be of use to them.

   b. To know if they hated you.

   c. To know if you should quit the business.

   d. To know if being an entrepreneur is worth it.

3. A good entrepreneur would _____ his or her faults if his or her actions bring adverse effect.

4. Going the extra mile helps to _____.

    a. gain more profit

    b. create the best value and please customers

    c. create a good ambiance for the customers

    d. create an enabling environment

5. Customers value _____ in your impression of yourself.

6. What should you intend to improve upon as an entrepreneur?

    _____
    _____
    _____
    _____

7. What is the yardstick of evaluating yourself?

   _____
   _____
   _____
   _____

8. What should your damage control method be?

   _____
   _____
   _____
   _____

CHAPTER 6

PRATICE PROFESSIONALISM

1. Professionalism requires that you are _____ and _____ with your work.

2. A good dress sense can make you _____ a deal or _____ a deal.

3. How do you handle internal issues with your staff?

   _____

   _____

   _____

   _____

4. One of the traits of being professional is _____.

   a. money-minded

   b. accountability

   c. business-oriented

   d. eloquence

5. How often do you keep in touch with your existing customers?

   _____
   _____
   _____
   _____

6. How do you uniquely relate with different kinds of customers?

   _____
   _____
   _____
   _____

7. How well your business thrives is based on _____.

   a. access to proper information

   b. access to funds

   c. access to loans

   d. access to friends and family

8. You can also get inspired on how well to maintain customer satisfaction by _____.

   a. reading the news

   b. advertising your business

   c. convincing them to buy your product

   d. reading life stories of successful businesses

Chapter 7

GOING THE EXTRA MILE

1. In a simple way, what does it mean to go the extra mile as an entrepreneur?

   _____

   _____

   _____

   _____

2. What was the first thing discussed as a visible sign of going the extra mile?

   a. Being passive.

   b. Being passionate.

   c. Wishing all goes well.

   d. Being nonchalant.

3. Give two examples of how to express your passion to serve your customers as an entrepreneur on a daily basis.

   _____
   _____
   _____
   _____

4. How can you describe "paying attention to details"?

   a. Making sure the tiniest details of your business are not left unattended.

   b. Verbalizing it.

   c. Looking out for profit.

   d. Ensuring your staff has a field day.

5. What examples were given in the chapter on paying attention to details? List 3 of them.

_____
_____
_____
_____

6. Do you agree that customers differ? What is the reason for your answer?

_____
_____
_____
_____

7. Do you believe that paying attention to your individual customer's taste and preference is possible?

_____
_____
_____
_____

8. Write out how you intend to practice individual customer satisfaction.

   _____

   _____

   _____

   _____

Chapter 8

SYSTEMS TO RETAIN CUSTOMERS

1. Are excitement and a big smile all that is needed to keep your customers coming back for more?

   _____
   _____
   _____
   _____

2. What is meant by "systems to retain customers"?

   _____
   _____
   _____
   _____

3. What are the two things that can be achieved when an entrepreneur keeps his or her customers happy and satisfied?

_____

_____

_____

_____

4. How many systems were discussed in the chapter?

    a. One.

    b. Two.

    c. Three.

    d. Four.

5. Which of the systems discussed is particularly for new customers?

_____

_____

_____

_____

6. Which system discussed is particularly for loyal customers?

___

7. How would an entrepreneur giving back to his or her community affect his or her brand image? Give a reason for your answer.

___

8. Why is getting regular feedback so important to an entrepreneur?

___

SYSTEMS TO RETAIN CUSTOMERS

Chapter 9

Continued Education

1. Why should continued education be important to an entrepreneur?

   _____

   _____

   _____

   _____

2. What are the two shades by which education is acquired?

   _____

   _____

   _____

   _____

3. Give one example each of a soft and a hard skill.

   _____

   _____

4. Do you agree that informal education can take place in very unlikely circumstances? Can you share an example with an experience where you learned something important through an informal setting?

5. How do reading books and articles help to improve your approach to business?

6. Are human relations a learned skill? Why is this so?

_____

_____

_____

_____

ANSWER KEY

NOTE: This answer key is prepared from the viewpoint of a reader who is running a food business. This approach makes it more subjective and easier to understand. Restaurants are used as the example but please replace your business in the example and apply the principals.

Chapter 1

1. The knowledge needed to build up my confidence to take my business to the next level as well as the guidelines to avoid pitfalls and stumbling blocks. The undiluted, unpolluted, and unfiltered truth.

2. crucial

3. Customers ought to be king. A business is built on the desire and the need to serve. Every decision made ultimately can be attributed to customer loss, retention, or incites referrals. As a

result, every decision made must have the needs and satisfaction of each customer in mind.

4. Lovers of food, food adventurists, and food junkies.

5. profits

6. Ensuring their needs are met and proactively avoiding conflict. We include exactly what the Customer ordered in their delivery. Communication is ensured at all times, and the customer is made to feel like he/she matters. We emphasis a smooth customer experience. Aside from the financial aspect, the major aim is to ensure the customer is pleased, the tastes and textures are consistent, and the best ingredients are used.

7. The customer is treated like royalty. Emphasis is made on ensuring everything the client requests is made available to him/her in an aesthetically pleasing manner.

ANSWER KEY

8. Lovers of food, food adventurists, and food junkies.

9. Love for food and creativity.

10. Maintaining good customer relationships. Having food cooked and delivered with the highest level of food safety and ensuring consistency in taste while providing a great product at a value price. Ensuring customers get their money's worth.

11. To be known by name as the best restaurant amongst my competitors. For example, if a restaurant is called Early to Rise and they specialize in breakfast, then they should want to be known for the best breakfast entrees in their area.

Chapter 2

1. dependent

   Profit is the only indication of a successful business. When the business thrives, more money is generated as a result of its success, therefore; the two go hand in hand.

2. A mix of both English breakfast dishes coupled with pastries and African dishes modernly packaged.

3. specialization and expertise

4. The menu list of foods that are made and delivered by the business.

5. Home delivery, middleman procurement of goods, and how-to training for aspiring chefs and food lovers.

6. Location. Where the business is situated matters as the living conditions and financial status of

the individuals living in that community will dictate the cost.

Competition. A survey would need to be carried out to know the general cost similar businesses are charging for the same or similar service.

Cost of purchase, production, and delivery are also factors that will contribute to the cost of the overall service being rendered.

7. Time management and efficiency. From its inception to its delivery, the foods are made with each customer in mind, tailored exactly as they requested.

8. Incentives include, sometimes, free delivery, promos, and discounts.

Chapter 3

1. Integrity, honesty, and transparency with both staff and customers alike. The needs of our customers are our priority.

2. commitment and dedication

3. commitment

4. The business sets out to outdo itself at every given opportunity. Ex: Arriving early every day to make sure the tone is set for the customers when they arrive so they feel more welcomed.

5. excellence

6. Improving time management skills, providing

   safer and more aesthetically pleasing packaging and expanding into new recipes.

7. critical thinking

8. Food being served is completely different from what is served in the business environment. The

provision of home delivery. Expanding into selling products outside of food.

9. Goals have been set and are checked daily to ensure the business is on track.

   A relationship is built with the customer, thereby facilitating friendship or common ground, making it easy to accommodate their views.

Chapter 4

1. Loyalty

2. Personalized service.

   Personalized service makes the customer feel appreciated as well as reinforces the principle of

   "The customer is king." Personalization of service makes customers feel they are the only ones that matter.

   Welcoming environment.

   We take care to ensure the work environment is both conducive and welcoming to both workers and customers. Our general atmosphere is geared to incite or elevate the mood of the customer.

   Continuous Improvement.

   The implementation of different ideas and innovations also tells customers that the

ANSWER KEY

business strives to think of new ways to please and satisfy them.

Feedback.

The use of feedback informs the business of the customers' experiences, thereby identifying potential challenges, opportunities for growth, or commending us on a job well done.

3. the customer and the business

4. Catering to each need of each customer. What works for person A might not work for person B.

5. A lot of care has to be given to each component of the business. Decorations and renovations are ways to make a business attractive and appealing to customers. Neatness and good customer relations also contribute to making a business appealing and attractive.

6. questions

7. feedback and personalization

8. There are numerous formal and informal ways to get feedback. The use of forms with detailed questions is a more formal approach. Directly asking the customers their thoughts and possible issues with the business or service is an informal way to solicit feedback.

9. Staying on top of our game. Marketing strategies, as well as advertisements and referrals from existing loyal customers, attract new customers. Social media is a powerful tool and a medium through which customer acquisition can be accomplished.

10. Calls, texts, or e-mails.

11. How well customers are treated (customer relation) and attitude towards correction and growth.

ANSWER KEY

12. Take it as a learning curve. View their feedback as the customer expressing what they do not like about your services to help you best please them.

13. It should not be overbearing yet convey a sense of value to the customer.

14. Continuously working on areas of improvement highlighted by customers as well as maintaining a high level of integrity.

15. Mediate between the two. The staff is corrected while the customer is apologized to. The staff is then educated, so they don't repeat the same mistake, should it be found they were at fault.

Chapter 5

1. The business is very open to the complaints of customers; therefore, calls, text, and social media have been available for customers to reach out with their feedback and share their customer experience.

2. To know if the service would be of use to them.

3. accept and correct

4. create value and please customers

5. honesty

6. Weighing the pros and cons. In a bid to satisfy the customer, the business tends to shoot itself in the leg by sometimes overreaching beyond its current capabilities.

7. The satisfaction of customers as well as the efficiency and smooth running of the whole service from preparation down to delivery.

What were the ratings from the feedback? Were the same complaints addressed?

8. Apologize and rectify the mistake with the business bearing the cost. Foresight into possible loopholes as well as potentially difficult clients.

Chapter 6

1. detailed and thorough

2. seal, lose

3. Internal issues are dealt with in the absence of customers. It is considered private and therefore dealt accordingly.

4. accountability

5. Not as much as the business should. There is inconsistency in this aspect.

6. By dealing with each customer as an individual. Each customer, including friends, is treated individually based on previous dealing with them or purely from a business-customer standpoint if a new customer.

7. Access to proper information.

8. Reading life stories of successful businesses.

ANSWER KEY

Chapter 7

1. Going the extra mile is simply to put oneself in the position of the customer and work towards excellent customer satisfaction and quickly remedying mistakes.

2. Being passionate

3. Punctuality and sensitivity. Being early and sensitive to.

   The slightest details are fruits of a business's passion.

4. Making sure the tiniest details of your business are not left unattended.

5. a) Cleanliness of the business environment.

   b) Informing customers ahead of time what new services are available.

   c) Informing customers when goods are out of stock.

6. Yes, customers differ.

Customers are fundamentally human beings, and human beings have varying tendencies and redeeming qualities. As a result, each individual has different preference as well as likes and dislikes, especially with food.

7. Very much so. The improvement in modern technology makes it very possible to have a detailed document or file for each customer and their preferences.

8. Creating a customer file documented regularly based on the customer's order history and preferences, thereby generating a means of identifying a customer's preference and preparing it prior to their arrival.

Chapter 8

1. No. The service, experience, as well as other factors matter that contributes to the satisfaction of the customer.

2. A default system in which by virtue of its incorporation, retains customers.

3. a) It creates loyal customers.

   b) It brings in new customers as a result of existing customers spreading the word about the business. They become advertisers.

4. Four.

5. Onboarding. This is like a tutorial where the customer is given an introduction or orientation as to what the business is about and how best to utilize the services being offered.

6. Customer Loyalty

7. People want to be associated with something good, noble, and great. Giving back to the

community can be seen as a good and noble thing to do, which reflects on the character of the business. Doing this wins the hearts of not only loyal customers but new customers as well.

8. Regular feedback can be seen as pointers leading the business into success. This is what lets the business know its standing and position in the hearts of its customers. Feedback can be the answer to why a business is doing well or not.

Chapter 9

1. There are a lot of lessons to be learned. No one is an island. The world is constantly evolving, and as such, the business should also move with the times to stay relevant and up-to-date.

2. Formal and Informal.

   Formal—this is an education that takes place within a confined space such as a classroom or online class.

   Informal—this is the opposite and can be acquired from friends and family members.

3. Soft: Customer relation.

   Hard: Computer programming.

4. Yes.

   While working and engaged with a customer, the customer narrated an aspect of his life that struck deep as it was fill with hard truths as well as lessons that were applicable to life and business. You never know when a customer will share information with you to make a connection and how much you can learn by listening.

5. There are numerous experiences one can learn from. Many entrepreneurs have documented their experiences and their mistakes, mistakes that can be avoided as a result of them sharing their journey in business.

6. Yes. Each customer is blessed with their own character and trait. It is imperative that businesses understand this in order to know best how to deal and interact with their customer base.

Thank you for purchasing this workbook. You have taken a new step towards understanding and learning about your business. Please share a copy with another business owner or new entrepreneur who you feel can benefit as well.

If you have any questions please email Theresa Hayes at Theresa.Hayes@yahoo.com.

For Speaking Engagements and Workshops contact us through the following ways:
Facebook @Theresacaseyhayes
Instagram @Teeceehayes

Please like and follow us. We greatly appreciate you leaving a review of this book wherever it was purchased. Thank you for your support.

www.ingramcontent.com/pod-product-compliance
Lightning Source LLC
Chambersburg PA
CBHW021509210526
45463CB00002B/962